# HOUSES
# AROUND THE WORLD

by LOUISE LEE FLOETHE

Illustrated by RICHARD FLOETHE

CHARLES SCRIBNER'S SONS · New York

*1 3 5 7 9 11 13 15 17 19 RD/C 20 18 16 14 12 10 8 6 4 2*

*Printed in the United States of America*
*Library of Congress Catalog Card Number 73-1331*
*SBN 684-13529-9 (cloth)*

This is the story of houses around the world. Not big houses. Not rich houses. But the houses of farmers and workers and hunters and herders; town people and country people.

On each page there is a house in a different land. Some of the houses are modern, but most are built exactly as they were a long, long time ago. By far the greatest number of people in the world, even today, live in homes without the comfort of running water, plumbing or refrigeration. Many houses still do not have electricity, and if they do, often there is just a single light bulb.

Many of the homes pictured here are made by the people who live in them. Sometimes neighbors or relatives help. In the more modern countries people can usually afford to have their houses built by hired carpenters, masons, plumbers and roofers.

Houses differ because of climate, the building materials at hand and the nature of the people who build them. But each is shelter against heat and cold and rain and wind. Each is a place to eat and sleep and raise a family.

This is a New England village. These homes were built by the Pilgrims almost three hundred years ago and are still lived in today. These early settlers came from England. They tried to make their new homes look like the brick, wood and thatched-roofed cottages they left behind. However, since there were so many trees in the New World, it was easier to build their homes entirely of wood. Right away, the houses looked American!

People like this kind of house so much that homes like these are still being built all over the country.

The Monterey house was first built in California by Spanish settlers. They used a mixture of styles and building materials.

They learned how to make walls of adobe—clay baked hard in the sun—from the Pueblo Indians. Flat-pitched roofs, with wide overhangs to shade the windows, were copied from houses in the south of Spain, where the climate is warm and dry, much like California. Later, when New England carpenters arrived, they added their own designs to doors, windows and moldings.

Many people today build modern homes in the old Monterey style.

Seminole Indians, living in the swampy Florida Ever-
glades, build their chickees up off the damp ground. Sharply
slanted roofs, made of overlapping palm fronds, shed even
the heaviest rains. The sides of the chickees are left open to
allow cooling breezes to pass through. Mosquito nets, at-
tached to the rafters, are dropped over the bedrolls at night.

Cooking is done in the cooking hut which is shared by
members of the village.

Many Navaho Indians living in the near-desert lands of the Southwest still build their six-sided hogans of clay and logs. The hogan is a one-room house. The floors are of dirt. The doorway is covered by a blanket.

Many Navahos are sheep and goat herders. In spring and summer they travel with their herds from one grazing place to another. On the move, they build shelters of saplings and brush. In fall they return to their hogans and stay for the winter.

Far, far to the north in the icy Arctic, Eskimos build igloos to shelter them against the fierce winds and snow of winter. As they follow the herds of reindeer and seals, they can stop whenever they want to and build a new igloo in a few hours.

Everyone in the family helps build the igloo. Mother and children help make and carry the snow blocks. The father begins the igloo by laying blocks in a circle. Then, standing inside the circle, he lays snow blocks round and round, sloping them in a little as he builds. When the igloo is finished it is shaped like a half ball. Now the father cuts a hole in the wall to let himself out. Then he makes a tunnel of snow leading to the hole. The family crawls through the tunnel to go in and out of their home.

Inside the igloo a sleeping platform of snow is made and covered with heavy skins. Skins are also hung on the walls and across the entrance. Seal oil lamps give both heat and light.

Town houses in the lovely city of Kyoto in Japan are hidden behind little walled-in gardens designed to look like country landscapes. A tiny stream trickling between dwarfed plants and curiously shaped stones gives the garden a feeling of space.

The house is built of wood along simple lines. It has a raised floor, sliding paper-paned walls and a great overhanging roof. Although parts of the house are Westernized with refrigerator, TV and such, most people still prefer the charm of the old Japanese home.

Inside the house, sliding walls allow for making rooms larger or smaller as needed. Shoes are left outside so as not to soil the tatami, a floor covering of woven straw. There are no chairs; people sit on the floor. When it is time to go to bed, quilts are spread on the tatami. In the morning the quilts are rolled up and put away.

Battaks, a group of people living in Sumatra, build interesting, high-gabled houses out of bamboo and thatch. They decorate the gables with wonderful designs woven of bamboo. The horned heads decorating the rooftops show how many animals were killed for the house-building feast.

The Battak house is built on stilts. The front door is reached by a ladder. Under the stilts, where firewood and farm tools are kept, pigs, chickens and little children run around freely.

Many families in southern China live aboard junks and sampans. Sometimes thousands of these houseboats are jammed side by side in harbors and rivers.

Fisherfolk live in the junks. During the day they sail out to sea searching for a catch.

The tiny sampans haul freight or serve as water taxis. The living quarters on the sampans are very crowded, and the matted roof often leaks. Small children must be watched carefully to prevent them from falling overboard.

By far the greatest number of Chinese people live in the country. They live in small villages, now usually communes, and share the work of farm or small factory. Village houses vary widely. Most of them have electricity (one bulb hanging from the ceiling), but running water is rare.

Here, in Shensi Province, villagers live in caves dug into the dry clay hills. These homes are cool in summer and easy to heat in winter.

Not far from the city of Bangkok in Thailand, rows of houses stretch along the sides of narrow waterways. The houses are built high on stilts so that they will stay dry during the floods of the rainy season.

The houses have wide verandas facing the water. Sampans glide by, selling food, charcoal and many other wares. Behind the houses are vegetable gardens and fruit trees.

Each house has its own spirit house, a white doll-sized temple with a red roof decorated with gold. Inside the spirit house is a small image of the guardian spirit of the home and several little statues of horses and elephants. Every day the family brings offerings of a candle, incense, little dishes of food and fresh flowers.

"May our guardian spirit bless our home," the family prays.

In India most people are farmers. They live in little villages and go out to their fields every morning to work.

Most of the houses in the village are built by the owners themselves. They usually build the walls of rocks, mud and cow dung. They make the walls thick so as to keep the house as cool as possible during the terribly hot summers. The slanted roofs are made of straw and reeds tied over a bamboo framework and shed all but the heaviest rains. Floors are made in two layers. The first layer is of stones and thick black mud mixed with wheat stems. Over this the women smooth a mixture of mud and cow dung.

Almost every house has an inner courtyard where most of the household work is done. The family also eats here. During the summer they sleep in the courtyard on woven webbed beds, called charpoys. Sometimes cattle, or even a camel, wander into the courtyard and make themselves at home.

In Russia there are not enough houses for all the people. In the cities several families are often crowded into one apartment. In order to have more places for people to live, the government is tearing down many of the small wooden city houses and putting up block after block of brick apartment buildings.

However, on the outskirts of Moscow the little wooden house behind its picket fence is still a common sight. Very tightly built, this kind of house can be kept comfortably warm during the very long, cold winters.

A village in Siberia looks much like an early Western American town. Since there is plenty of lumber, all the houses are built of wood. Skilled ax-men join the logs tightly together to keep out the fierce winter blizzards. Corrals and barns are built close by.

In summer, the men herd the communal livestock far across the grassy steppes, setting up camps at night. Women and small children and some of the older men stay behind to care for the winter homes and to grow hay and potatoes.

Most people in Iran live in small farm villages. They build their own cottages from bricks of sun-dried clay. The roofs are flat, made of wood beams interlaced with willow branches and rushes. The top of the roof is filled in with dirt and smoothed down with a roller.

Usually the houses have only one room. Very few have glass windows. The house is dark when the doorway is covered. In winter the mother builds a small dung fire in the center of the room. She places a stool over the smoldering

dung with a blanket spread tent-like around it. The family sit in a circle and tuck their legs under the blanket to keep warm.

Every house has a courtyard. Cooking is done here. At night the farm animals—a donkey, sheep, oxen, a cow and chickens—are safe within the walls.

Water to fill the household water jars is dipped up from the stream which runs through the middle of the village. The stream is also used for bathing, washing clothes and irrigating the fields and gardens.

Many Englishmen feel that their little rustic cottages grouped together on a village lane are the homiest houses in the world.

Roofs are made of straw and last up to twenty or thirty years. Hazelwood strips, called spars, are pegged into the roofs around the eaves and at the ridgepole, the very top of the roof. The spars help to keep the thatch from blowing off during a storm. Casement windows are made of small leaded panes of glass. There are fireplaces in almost every room.

Nestling in pretty gardens, with roses and honeysuckle climbing the chimney walls, the little thatched cottages have a fairytale look.

Many of the farmhouses in northern Germany and parts of Denmark are hundreds of years old. The sharply pointed roofs are made of red tile. Brightly colored plaster walls are crisscrossed with black painted beams.

These houses are in two parts with a door between — one

part for the animals, the other for the farmer and his family. This makes it easy for the farmer to watch over his animals when the snow lies deep outside. Hay is stored on the second floor, where it is convenient to reach. It also helps keep the house warm in winter.

High up in the valleys of the Swiss Alps, cattle and goat herders live in sturdy wood chalets. Roofs slant steeply to better shed the deep snows of winter. Broad overhangs keep the snow from piling too high close to the house. Heavy slabs of slate or stone weight the roof down against strong mountain winds.

In summer the balconies across the front of the chalets are bright with geraniums.

Many people love the chalet style. They build houses like these even in mild climates. They buy cuckoo clocks shaped like little chalet houses.

This is a hilltop village in the south of Spain. The people who live here are farmers. Wheat fields, vineyards, olive groves and vegetable gardens grow in the valley below.

Most of the village houses are two stories high with red tiled roofs. Colorful flower boxes are at the front windows. Pigeons fly in and out of the dovecotes hanging on outside walls. Each house has a courtyard at the back with outer buildings for chickens, pigs, goats and ducks.

The front door opens into a wide stone-paved passage-way big enough for a mule cart to pass through. The living room and kitchen are downstairs. These rooms have tile floors and gleaming whitewashed walls. Bedrooms are up-stairs, and at the back is a big room where hay, potatoes, wheat and beans are stored.

In the old walled-in city of Kano in Nigeria, home builders decorate roofs with turrets pointing upward like giant thumbs. Clay is dug from nearby pits and made into cone-shaped bricks. Walls are made from these bricks piled many layers thick, strengthened with palm logs and then plastered

with mud. Every dry season the walls must be replastered and repaired.

Tin gutters stick out over the walls like guns. During the rainy season water must be drained quickly off the flat roofs or the houses would melt into big mud puddles.

A N'debele village in South Africa is a splash of color in a sea of gray-brown brush.

The men of the village start the building of the houses by making a round latticework of wooden poles and a thatched roof of river grasses. Then the women take over and wall in the latticework with a mixture of clay and cow dung. Court-

yards are built all around the huts, which the women decorate with bold, brilliant designs.

Every woman wants her house to be the most beautiful. She even makes designs on the floor of her courtyard. After heavy rains she paints her house and walls again, sometimes making all new designs.

On the tropical island of Grenada in the West Indies, many people live in two-story wooden houses built close to the beach or up the sides of green hills. Each house is painted a different color. A little balcony runs around the second floor. The windows have shutters so rooms can be darkened during the heat of the day. The tin roof is peaked to shed heavy rains.

Like their ancestors of long ago, the Maya Indians of Yucatán still build an oval, one-room house without windows. Each long side of the house has a door. The framework is made of saplings plastered with mud and then painted or whitewashed. The roof is thatched with palm leaves and grass. The floor is of dirt packed hard. Cooking, eating and visiting are usually done in the neatly raked courtyard.

Tall apartment buildings are sprouting up in South American cities. There are also many handsome new houses of modern design. Each homeowner tries to make his house different from his neighbors'. Wooden front doors, strikingly carved, and original mosaic designs on outside walls are greatly admired.

Many people in South America, coming from the country to the city hoping to find a better life, end up living in crowded shanty neighborhoods. Rickety shacks made from scraps of lumber, tin and cardboard cover the steep slopes. Sometimes during heavy rains the poor little shacks slide down the hillside, leaving families homeless.

People living in pleasant modern homes find it difficult to realize that so many people of the world still live in houses that are no better than huts.

Sometimes a primitive house is comfortable and suits the climate and living conditions of the land very well. But more often than not, a primitive house is crowded, dark and unsanitary.

Unfortunately, even in our big modern cities there are still dwellings that are dark, crowded and unsanitary.

Nevertheless, today more people than ever before in the history of man are housed reasonably well. Hopefully, someday everyone in every land will be able to live in cheerful, attractive houses suitable to their way of life.